Voices of Clay

by T. Borregaard
illustrated by Linda Graves

EDUCATORS PUBLISHING SERVICE
Cambridge and Toronto

Series Authors: Kay Kovalevs and Alison Dewsbury
Series Consultant: Melinda Rice
Commissioning Editors: Sarah Russell, Bonnie Lass, and Sethany Rancier Alongi
Senior Editorial Manager: Sheila Neylon
Text by T. Borregaard
Edited by Anne McKenna and Wendy Drexler
Designed by Jennifer Johnston
Illustrated by Linda Graves

Making Connections program developed by Educators Publishing Service, a division of School Specialty Publishing and by Harcourt Education, a division of Reed International Books Australia Pty Ltd

ISBN 0-8388-3341-1

2010 2009 2008 2007 2006
10 9 8 7 6 5 4 3 2 1

Printed in China

Contents

Introduction

The book you are about to read—*Voices of Clay*—is a fictional story. However, it is about an ancient group of people that once existed—the Anasazi. *Anasazi* is a Navajo word used to describe these people. We don't know what the Anasazi called themselves. They lived in the southwest of the United States for about two thousand years.

The Anasazi lived for many years in sandstone houses. They built their special houses along the overhanging canyon walls of an enormous plateau in an area in southwest Colorado. Today this area is part of a national park.

Around the fourteenth century, the Anasazi people suddenly abandoned their clifftop sandstone houses and moved south. No one knows why they moved. Perhaps it was because of drought. The drought described in *Voices of Clay* is only one of many theories explaining why the Anasazi left.

Another mystery of the Anasazi people is that when they abandoned their beautiful sandstone cities, they also abandoned their pottery technology. Even though the people went to live in new settlements further south, they never again made the painted glazewares described in *Voices of Clay*.

Chapter 1
Wind Song

Catori awoke, hoping the winds had changed. Every morning she awoke with that thought in her head. She lay still for a moment, wide-eyed, staring up into the gloom of the sandstone room. Her stomach rumbled. She was hungry, but she knew she wouldn't get any breakfast. There wasn't much food around these days. She sighed as she inched out of the warm furs like some strange beast shedding its skin.

She dressed in the long, loose skirt and fitted top that all women of the cliffs wore.

The heavily embroidered patterns around the hem and neckline weighed the fabric down against the winds. When she left the stone doorway of her family house, there they were—still singing their hot, dry song. For too many years, the north winds had sung their song for the rift valley. Always the same tune in the same beat, over and over. Catori was weary of it.

She made her way through the buildings of Aponvi. They were carved directly into the sandstone cliff, about halfway up. All the villages of the rift valley dwellers were built this way, so that there was no way to climb down to them from above, and only one way to reach them from below. It was a safety measure from long ago, when there had been enemies. There were no enemies now, except the wind.

Catori walked around the sacred circle that marked the top of the huge underground kiva, the round structure used for ceremonies. In the old days, the kiva would have been filled with offerings to the gods, but there was nothing to spare anymore, not even for the gods.

At the edge of the cliff Catori stood and watched the sun rise over the distant blue-green horizon. The cliff on the opposite side of the rift cast long shadows on the valley floor. Aponvi was built on the sunset side of the rift valley so that it always caught the first rays of dawn.

Ignoring the winds, Catori hitched her skirt up and climbed down the cliff face. She could have done it in the dark, so familiar were the handholds and footholds. In fact, she had climbed down in the dark many times. She'd climbed down nearly every day since she was old enough to walk. It was the only way to and from the village.

The cliff face was constantly in use as the villagers brought up food and water from the valley below. Harvesting and hunting were done down in the rift, where the shiny river slid like a silver fish from an unknown source to an unknown destination.

Like everyone else, Catori spent her days in the valley, but she was neither a farmer nor a hunter. She provided the village with something else: the means to cook and carry the food others harvested or hunted, and more often the means to trade with other villages. Catori was a potter.

She walked toward a small mud potter's hut near the bank of the river. The hut provided shelter from the hot sun and a place to keep the tools and the pottery as it dried. The wet river clay was far too heavy to carry up to the village. It was easier just to work next to the source.

CHAPTER 2

The Village Awakens

CATORI STOPPED and turned back to look behind her. In the village, the others were beginning to awaken. Men, women, and children crept out of the dark holes of doorways in the stone.

In the early light, the sandstone glowed, striped by great bands of yellow, orange, and red. Though the day was just beginning, Catori thought the colors and light looked more like day's end. The stone had a feeling of finality to it, as though it was getting old and tired.

Catori sighed sadly and turned back to continue on her way. She passed through the long rows of corn. There were fewer and fewer harvests each year. The plants themselves were shriveled and dwarfed, and the corncobs were far too small. All of the plants leaned in the same direction, crippled by the constant winds.

When Catori reached the potter's hut, Chochmo was already working. He looked up and nodded curtly. Chochmo was always curt these days. Two months ago, the constant winds had driven his wife into madness.

Catori shook her head. He should have known better than to take a wife off the plains. She would have had a hard enough time getting used to the cliff life, even without the winds. With the winds, she didn't stand a chance. No one born outside the rift valley could stand their constant song.

Chochmo wore the customary loincloth tied about his waist. The white fabric was already covered in orange clay smudges. His fingers never stopped moving. A pot was taking shape in his hands. He was making a huge cooking pot.

Chochmo coiled long snakes of clay around and around, pressing them together rhythmically. The rest of his body was so still it was as though his fingers operated independently.

"That pot will be a lot for me to paint," Catori remarked.

"You like the big ones, more room to experiment with new designs," Chochmo replied, without looking up from his work.

Catori didn't argue with him—he was right. She gathered a small pot of black paint and several cactus spine brushes. She selected a large bowl from the huge collection of pots she'd made over the past week. Then she went outside. She did not like to work inside the dim, shadowed hut.

Outside though, she had to deal with the winds. They would tear the brush from her hand if she wasn't careful. Sometimes the winds even tried to take the pot itself. It was no wonder the never-ending, hollow scream of air through the canyon drove so many people away, and so many others insane.

But Catori was nowhere near madness—anger sometimes, but not madness. It wasn't even the winds that angered her. It was the stubbornness of those who stayed. Catori looked up at Aponvi and saw only decay. It was long past the time they should have left the cliffs and the rift valley. They needed to find a new home where people would bc happy, where there were no hot winds bringing famine and death with them.

Very few crops grew in the valley anymore. The north winds were not rain bringers. They sang only of heat, and of drought, and of barren soils. They could not be blamed for this, for they came from the desert and that was all they knew. Catori was not angry with them, she was angry with the fact that her world was dying and only she seemed to see it.

The rest of the village insisted on staying. The villagers had lost all hope that the winds would change, and yet they refused to seek change for themselves. Catori was willing to leave her home but she was not willing to leave her people, even if it meant starving alongside them.

Catori bent over her work. The heat of the wind made her shirt stick to her back. More and more, the villagers relied on trading her pottery for the necessities of life.

Catori was one of the best painters in the entire rift valley. Many outsiders came just to trade for pots she had decorated. She began to decorate her pots with hope. She put her feelings into the geometric black-and-white designs. She sent her pots away as symbols of encouragement. Some of them told stories of better places and better things. Others, darker, told of death if they stayed.

Catori leaned back against the outside wall of the hut and dipped her brush into the black paint. The winds pushed against her, and she turned her face into them. Sometimes she tried to paint that pattern onto her pots: symmetrical swirls and lines of endless songs sung by endless winds. She painted the winds as a force driving people away. She painted them as a reason to leave.

Everyone in Aponvi loved Catori's pots. The graceful designs reminded them that there was something else beyond the wind. The images spoke of places to travel and beautiful things to see. Her designs gave them hope, and there was precious little hope left for the people of the cliffs.

Late that afternoon, Catori sat in the shade of the hut, facing away from her village. Periodically she would glance at the river in front of her. The water had drawn back from the banks, leaving wide areas of drying mud.

Sometimes, Catori would look farther up and across the rocks and sparse plants that covered parts of the valley floor. She would spot a branch on a dead shrub that curved a certain way. It would become part of her design, a repeated shape, drawn from nature and living once more in black pigment on a white background.

For Catori that little branch spoke. It repeated over and over one single sentence: "Go—go now, before it is too late."

Looking up for new inspiration, she saw something halfway up the far cliff face, way off to her left just before the valley curved out of sight. It looked like a star flashing, blinking from the cliff. She knew instantly what it was.

Chapter 3

Warning!

Catori stood. The pot fell from her hands and shattered at her feet. She stepped forward, unaware that her feet crushed a fragment of dry, unfired clay into dust.

Just as Catori drew a breath to shout the alarm, someone behind her saw the same flashing star and yelled, "The war beacon! The war beacon is shining!" The farmers in the field dropped their hoes and tilling sticks and began to run toward Aponvi.

Catori dashed inside the potter's hut for Chochmo.

"Hurry, Chochmo. We have to go."

Chochmo looked up, annoyed. He was working on the most delicate part of the pot—the finely curved rim. "Why are you interrupting me? It's not dinnertime yet."

Catori shook her head. "Someone is flashing the war beacon."

"Don't be ridiculous, that old thing hasn't been used in decades. Well, at least not since the last war."

"It is being used now."

"Which one?"

"Qaletaqa's beacon, from the south."

"And what's the message?"

"How should I know? I never learned the code."

Chochmo, who did not like to be interrupted, especially by war, stood and stretched.

"I learned it." He stuck his head out the hut door and looked to the left, toward the cliff village of Qaletaqa far, far away across the rift valley.

The beacon system had been set hundreds of years ago, when raiders had visited the rift regularly. The cliff dwellers had been prosperous, and there had been more to steal back then. The villages normally had little to do with one another, but they soon discovered that in times of war it was best to band together.

Thus each village used a smooth metal disk to reflect the sun's rays at the nearest villages across the rift. The system was set up as one long chain, so villages miles and miles away at one end of the rift valley could send warnings or requests to villages all the way at the other end. Messages flashed from one beacon to the next.

The endless north winds had brought drought with them, but they had also brought peace. For now there was little left to steal, and the cliff dwellings were too difficult to conquer merely for the sake of conquering. The beacons had not been needed in years.

Chochmo squinted across the distance and mouthed silently to himself with the flashes of light. Catori marveled at this speech without sound. Then she thought of her pottery painting and realized that it, too, was a type of soundless speech.

"It's not war. They want a council."

Catori frowned. "Why? This isn't the trading time."

"Not just Qaletaqa. The villages, all of them, all the way along the valley."

"Where?"

"Here, of course. We are the mid-point. It's the most convenient place and they all know of us because of your pottery. It draws people."

"Do they say why we're to have the council?"

"No, but we can all guess."

Catori said, "The winds."

Chochmo nodded and went back into the pottery hut. He had an urn to finish.

Catori did not go back to work. Instead she headed after the others toward the cliff.

By the time Catori had reached the carved sandstone of her home, the village was buzzing with facts she already knew. There were others, older than Chochmo, who also remembered how to read the beacon's light. Now everyone knew of the council.

"How long do we have?" Catori asked no one in particular.

"A month, no more," an elderly man replied. He remembered the old days when people traveled the length of the rift to trade goods. He knew how long it took to travel to the village.

"I hope they bring their own food," grumbled a young woman.

"They'll have to," Catori replied. "We simply haven't enough to feed them all."

Someone else asked, "Don't we get a say in this?"

Catori shrugged. "What can we do? We can't refuse to receive them."

"You'll have to make more pots, Catori," said the village headman as he came up behind her, his face wrinkled with concern. "This is an opportunity we must take advantage of. We won't get a chance to trade like this again."

Catori looked at him. "I'm doing as much as I can. We need more help in the pottery hut. You've taken all my best helpers away to hunt and harvest."

The headman glared at her tone. "You forget your place. You are still only a potter."

Catori sighed.

"My place has nothing to do with it. Either you'll give me the help I need, or you'll get less pottery," she explained calmly.

The headman was not stupid. "You will get your help, starting tomorrow." Catori nodded and turned away to climb back down the cliff. There was still a little daylight left and she had pots to paint.

Catori got her help. Young men and women came to coil bowls and urns and coat the outsides with white slip, but only she did the decoration. Only she painted the firm black lines that spoke of leaving it all behind.

A few weeks later, people from the other villages began to arrive. The people of Aponvi had thought the beacon spoke of messengers. They were wrong. Entire villages of men, women, and children came with all they could carry. They set up camp in the valley below and waited. By the end of the month, everyone who was going to come to the council had arrived.

CHAPTER 4

A New Beginning

CATORI WAS NOT important enough to sit on the council, but so many of the visitors had asked about her that Aponvi's headman included her because her pottery was so well known. Some even said the pots spoke to them.

"Do you see this one?" One headman showed his tiny clay perfume bottle proudly. "It tells me of green fertile lands, where great beasts roam, and crops grow strong."

The headman of Aponvi shook his head. "It is just a pot. It cannot speak."

"And yet the war beacon is but a flash of light, and it spoke loudly enough to bring us all together," Catori said softly.

"Can we get on with the council?" the headman said, giving her a harsh look. "We must do something about this wind. The heat is killing our crops and destroying our lands."

"We cannot control the wind," said the headman of Qaletaqa.

Catori reached behind her and brought forward a huge cooking pot. The designs across its surface were nothing more than geometric black shapes on a white background. Nevertheless, inside that design the headmen of the council saw pictures.

The pictures showed long lines of figures walking away from the rift valley and the sandstone cliffs. People were walking away from the wind, carrying only what they needed to survive. They saw baskets of seed that would become fields of corn and squash. They saw herds of great beasts to be hunted far away. They saw new buildings of stone, pieced together above the earth rather than cut into the cliffs.

"It is time we left," said one headman.

"What is holding us here?" asked another.

"Only our history, our houses, our homes," replied the headman of Aponvi.

"We will make new history," said Catori.

"We can build new houses," said the headman of Qaletaqa.

"No home is worth starving for," Catori added.

They all fell silent for a long time, staring at Catori's pot. The pot spoke to them without words. They listened.

Catori and the people of Aponvi left their village the very next day. They filled baskets with provisions—the seeds and tools they would need to build new homes—but they left much of Catori's pottery behind because it was too heavy. Behind them, the sandstone cliffs were empty except for the hot north winds blowing through.

The villages traveled together, south along the valley floor. After months of traveling through deserts and rolling plains, they found their land of green fields. There the rain fell freely, and the north winds did not blow.

They resettled their way of life in a new village and continued much as they had before, only happier, and with bigger bellies. The hunters hunted buffalo. The farmers grew corn, squash, and beans. Catori, however, never made another pot.